How to Own and Operate A Nano-Brewery

By Dan Woodske

1

About the Brewer (and writer of this fine book)

Hi, I'm Dan Woodske and I own and operate Beaver Brewing Company in lovely Beaver Falls Pennsylvania with my equally beautiful wife Kimberly and my best friend Bemus, who is a 5 year-old male cat.

If you've never heard of the brewery it wouldn't surprise me. Since it is only a 1 BBL system I work with (that's a 31 gallon capacity) I distribute within a tight radius from my brewery and sell quite a bit of the beer on site.

I also consider a nano-brewery to be anything 3 BBL's or under...however I designed this book so if you were opening a 300 BBL brewery, or any business for that matter, it will be beneficial to you.

I like to think I run an artisan nano-brewery that focuses on off the wall styles and beers. You'll learn about a few of them as I shamelessly promote the beer throughout the book...well only a few times, I'll number them for you and keep it below 10...

So how the hell did I get to own a nano-brewery? I started working in politics. After about 6 years some of the people I worked with were indicted and went to prison. I've always been pretty adverse to prison myself, so I bounced around in marketing jobs a bit 'til I settled on Beaver Brewing Company. I have always been in sales, marketing, or PR so I will always come back to stories that relate to my background when I need to fill up some pages...

You'll notice that I'm not going to tell you your idea or any idea is stupid. I've heard that enough times myself and I am sure you will as you move forward, so no need to pile on. I am also not one of those aloof business owners that says "I did it, I am smart, and if you don't do it this way it will fail."

I'm here to offer you real life business information that could help you along the way of starting a nano-brewery, or it will let you know that you should turn and run like hell...

Whatever you decide, enjoy the journey!

Writers Note: You lucky dog! This is the second volume of the book and has some more info that you will find useful...I said to myself if I get over 100 emails with questions about the book I will re-edit it and add some info that people were asking about...it took 47 days to get 100 emails! It took me some time but I added a bit more insight on what people asked the most...hope it helps!

I also wrote another book, Nanobrewery U.S.A. that chronicles Nano's across the country. I'll add some of the info I learned from them into this book as well.

Introduction

Wow - page five already. You're almost ready to brew!
So you want to start a nano-brewery? I am sure if you are
reading this book you have already learned from friends,
family, message boards, and anyone else listening to your
dream of a operating a nano-brewery that the idea is
stupid, it can't work, and you'll never make money.

I can say that I totally agree with them…if you do it the
wrong way. I have read from "experts" that running a
nano-brewery is a money pit that can't be done with
equipment/materials costs. I can tell you from personal
experience it *IS* possible to do it profitably. You just have
to be creative and willing to work. If you do neither of
these, please put down the book and continue on with
your life…

Great! You are at the very least creative or willing to work
so you can continue on with this journey in nano-brewing.
I'm going to tell you what I have done, what has worked,
what has blown up in my face, and what you can expect
on your path to brewing beer.

We will start with what you'll need before you even start
your brewery and touch on every aspect of running your
brewery. So grab your favorite brew and prepare to
begin your odyssey into!

Here are a few things in this book...REAL life brewery experience. I try to sprinkle in a few REAL stories about things that actually happened to the brewery and the business and how you can benefit from my experience.

A few things NOT in the book...

How to brew beer. You won't find anything in here about that. If you are reading this and don't know how to brew beer, put this down and buy a homebrew book; you will thank me later.

Also not included is a step-by-step process on what exact items you need to do to open a nanobrewery. This is not a science project, shit happens and not everything goes in order. You may also be a super genius that is able to skip things I talk about.

First a quick story about KVASS...

I feel it is important to tell a short story that will drive home a few points. Those points are:

1. Know your market

2. Learn from your mistakes.

3. Enjoy your success.

Do you even know what Kvass is? If you didn't grow up in Russia I doubt it. I call it the Russian Health Drink of the 11th century. Traditional Kvass is made of 3 main ingredients (other than water): Bread, Lemons, and Raisins. People figured out pretty early in history that if you didn't get Vitamin C you'd lose your teeth. (Damn that scurvy!)

Without sugar cane lemonade was out of the question. So Russians would crush their old bread into a container, squeeze some lemons over it, add some raisins (as a sweetener), and pour warm water over it. The yeast in the bread would ferment the sugars from the lemons and the raisins to produce a very low alcohol, slightly carbonated, refreshing "health" drink.

Breweries generally don't make it because honestly, who the hell wants a beer with less than 2% alcohol?

I set off with Beaver Brewing Company looking to not only to make great beer, but to offer beer to people who may never have experienced it before. I actually got the idea for Kvass from my beer nerd friend Buck who wanted to try every style of beer made. Yes...he is THAT GUY.

This was early in my goings on as a brewer but I had already set the bar for off the wall beers and wanted to keep it going...So I made my Kvass as traditionally as I could...Bread, Lemons, Raisins, touch of malt and the lowest amount of hops possible to still classify it as "Beer".

I promoted the hell out of it. The internet, at bars, at tastings, festivals, and growler sales....anyone that would listen to me knew the release date for my Kvass. And when it was released it was a crazy success. I sold more of that in one day of growler sales at the brewery then I ever had of all my beers combined. It was completely sold out. 3 people actually walked out with sixtels of the Kvass to tap into their kegerators at home. It even became the #1 Kvass in the world according to a popular beer review website. I figured I was the new "Kvass King" and I could maybe start a whole Kvass line. (Writers Update: Since the first run of this book "The Bros" at *BeerAdvocate® Magazine* rated the Kvass in Issue #66 calling it "An Amazing brew".)

I do my growler sales monthly so I prepared myself for the next month by making Kvass non-stop. I had tons of it (for a nano-brewery) on hand and was ready to keep on pimping it out. The next month came and I was surprised again...almost no one bought that damn Kvass. I literally cut the price in half the 2nd day of growler sales hoping to get a few more buyers. It got to the point that I was giving it away (since it is low alcohol the Kvass does not keep a fresh taste very long).

So what happened? The people who drank the Kvass said they loved it. I know this because I MAKE everyone try all the beer I have at the brewery to see what they like the most and all the feedback was great. So again, what the Hell happened?

Let's get back to those three points...

1. Know Your Market

I knew the patrons of Beaver Brewing appreciated new crazy style beers, but what I didn't know was that they constantly wanted new experiences. The Kvass was cool, but after you have it...you have it. You want what is next. I also learned that regardless of taste, beer drinkers actually want alcohol in their beer. My Kvass tops out at 1.6% ABV. Like I said, it's traditional. I have had 4%-5% ABV kvass style beers and they are great, but not what I wanted. I want you to taste Mother-Russia when you are drinking mine. I failed to understand that my market was made up of beer drinkers who wanted a constant new experience. When planning your beer, figure out what the people of your area want, and meet those needs.

2. Learn from your mistakes

I quickly found out that I didn't need that much Kvass on hand at any given time. I do however keep it year-round at the brewery because it does have a fan base and there are always a few "Noobs" that want to give it a try. I also learned that I better research new recipes on a regular basis to fill the needs of my customers.

3. Enjoy your success

So the Kvass was a one hit wonder. But it does get me noticed. You won't find many (and possibly no other) breweries making Kvass year-round. My version was even rated the #1 Kvass in the world according to a few popular beer review websites. People still kick the tires on the Kvass at the brewery and it's always fun to watch people try it for the first time because they have no idea what to expect. I also gained plenty of new regular customers from the Kvass who otherwise would have never come to the brewery.

Your "Kvass story" could be completely different. You may make a new beer and your regulars will ask "What the hell happened to your "blank" beer? Why isn't it here? That was my favorite!" Moral of the story is always ask for feedback from your patrons and try to understand what they are looking for from your brewery. Most importantly, find outwhat will make them come back to your brewery.

Before You Start...

Don't pick up the federal permit and start filling it out as quickly as possible. Think for a minute, maybe even two. I actually want you to get a pen out and write in this book (if it is a shared book please refrain from this, but write it down in your head). What are your expectations in running a brewery?

Some answers you may have written down: Make money, make great beer, build a base of customers so you can open a larger brewery, have fun with friends selling your beer around town, retire, I have no idea.

None of these are wrong answers but you really need a destination before you start. I have talked to many nano-brewers out there and I have heard all of these answers and all were successful at achieving them. The nano-brewers I have talked to who opened and closed quickly seemed to have no direction. They opened hoping they would find that direction but never did.

Whatever answer you have chosen I want you to make every decision on building your brewery associated with that goal. If it is making money please focus on your costs. Keep them low and forecast before you spend.

If it was about making great beer focus on your recipes before you jump into brewing. Have your "flagship" beer perfected and ready to hit the market as soon as you can.

I personally looked at building a base of customers with the plans of opening a larger brewery or a brew pub. Instead of investing all my time and money into a large system that I had no idea how to run in an industry I was clueless in I figured I would start small and then see if I could or would want to do it more.

Also, take some time to think about where you are located. Most importantly, what state you are located in. State laws vary wildly from state to state. In Pennsylvania where I am located you can expect your brewery license to be around $1,450. The excise taxes for beer in PA is about .42 cents a sixtel sold. In Virginia, you can expect a brewery license to run you about $2,150. Ohio runs nearly $4,000.

This annual cost could drastically change your goals before you start. Can you cover those licensing costs? Do you care? A quick check on your state's licensing authority will give you some sanity on this subject.

Also think about distribution...are you in a state that allows you to distribute your beer? You may have to go through a wholesaler.

Do you only want to sell your product on site? Make sure you are allowed. Some states require additional licenses to sell growlers on site.

Do you want to go the brewpub direction? If yes, look into your state's laws for selling beer on site for consumption.

How much time do you have to invest? You can always get more money, but never more time. If you think you are pressed for time now, opening a nano-brewery will not give you more free time.

I want you to ask yourself these questions before you continue to read. They will greatly shape your thinking as we move forward and give you that "Direction" we were talking about earlier.

Let's start...

Don't grab that damn form and start filling it out! We're still not there. What's your favorite brewery? I am sure it has a name. Start thinking of one, but don't exhaust all your efforts around it. I consulted one would-be brewer who wouldn't go forward with his plan until he had a name for his brewery. I emailed him 6 months after we met to make sure he was moving along, he said he was still working on the name....I left him alone after that.

You do want to make sure that name isn't taken and doesn't infringe on any copyrights and/or trademarks. A quick search on the US Trademark Office website should give you a good idea. Another quick and dirty way to help you out is to type it in on a search engine...do you get any hits? Try typing the name into social media sites too.

While the name shouldn't hold you back, you need to have one. And since you are a nano-brewer you can instantly gain some name recognition if your brewery has a local theme attached to it. You won't be distributing in 12 states anytime soon so don't be afraid to keep it local. Mine is named after the County my brewery is based in, Beaver. There is a lot of local pride in Western Pennsylvania and people like to support their neighbors.

Whatever you decide make sure you can live with it...forever! Once you have it down it's going to be costly and time consuming to change it.

Next, start thinking about what type of beer you are going to make...Ales, Lagers, High Alcohol, Fruit, Wheat, Sour, Gluten Free, or maybe even a world class Kvass (shameless self promotion #2). Depending on the style or styles of beer you make you will need to get different equipment and that may change your costs. We will get into that later.

I personally wanted to focus on bringing people a new beer experience with every beer they ever tried from Beaver Brewing. I didn't want them to fall in love with one beer, I wanted them to fall in love with the entire brewery. Its fun coming into the brewery because you never know what is coming. It isn't "Insert Hop" single-hopped-IPA when you come into my place. You'll find Citra Sauvin Wheat, or Basil, maybe the Nelson Sauvin Pale Ale or even the Chamomile Wheat.

This gets back to knowing your market...have a game plan...but be ready to change on a dime. You could always be wrong.

Start brewing beer. After you brew a few really good batches go back and brew some more. Right after that I would probably recommend brewing a few more...get the point? You'll probably say I have been brewing for 10 years, I know what I am doing. You very well may, but have you brewed 4 batches in a week...for 12 months straight? You may be that busy with your operation; until you brew frequently you won't know if you are up for it or not.

I have also consulted with "brewers" that haven't brewed beer. I shit-you-not that 3 guys came to me for a consulting session and I talked to them for about 30 minutes and asked them what they brewed, they answered "Nothing". Nothing? Really? They said they would learn when they got their license. While that model may work, I would highly recommend brewing at least 1 batch before you start. Also brew some beers and styles you never have brewed before. If you make a great IPA challenge yourself and make a Roggenbier. Try to expand your horizons so you can change your beers up if you find the market doesn't like your flagship beer. Speaking of Roggenbier I make one, and people at the brewery love it...if you want some homework figure out what the beer is and make one.

I actually have 3 "flagship" beers and they all came from me experimenting. The *I.Porter.A* - A beer made with Porter Malts and IPA style hops. *Chamomile Wheat* – Witbier made with a healthy amount of Chamomile Flowers and *Basil* – An Amber Ale brewed with a pound of fresh basil in each batch. I offer each of them year-round and the Basil has been the #1 seller since day one.

Up to this point you are probably saying to yourself that this dumbass hasn't told me one thing about actually opening a nano-brewery...What equipment do I need? What licenses do I need to have? I am trying to prepare you for that by building a foundation for what you want to do...whatever that goal may be.

Most importantly, and I beg of you, before you do anything...please write this down. I want you to ask yourself a very simple question: "How much money am I willing to lose?" Not MAKE....but LOSE. This could totally blow up in your face. Could you and your family get by if you lost $5,000...how about $20,000? Is the number $500? Whatever it is, you HAVE to know that going in. No matter how much people try to change it, this still is America...the land of opportunity. With that opportunity comes risk, and with risk there is failure. This may not work so please prepare yourself AND your family in the case that it does not.

I constantly blurt out this stat when consulting people because I KNOW this question will be asked, "Do you think this will work?" My answer is no, statistically speaking it probably won't. Over 70% of small businesses created in 2001 did not exist in 2010. So if you are playing by the odds it won't work...with that said you are smart, I mean you did buy this book so you're already way ahead of the game! But seriously, please make plans for this NOT working. I don't want you living out of your car drinking homebrew and yelling at passers-by "This stuff is awesome! It's your loss!"

And one last thing...the business plan. I went to school for business, and a good one at that. I can tell you the business plan for me was worthless. But for others it works as a Bible. Poke around on the internet, read a few. If you think it is worthwhile, take the time and fill it out. While writing a full plan wasn't for me, I thought about the brewery on a daily basis. How much money do I have? What beers will I make? Who can I sell to? I didn't WRITE the plan, but if you asked me any relevant question about my business one year before I opened, I could have answered it for you. Moral of the story...make a plan that works for you and/or your partners...

If you plan on asking people other than family for money you will NEED a business plan. The whole "I got this great idea" doesn't get you too far when applying for a loan or asking for money from strangers. We'll get into funding later but a plan of some sort is necessary no matter how it is accomplished.

Before we move on I want to share a story since I mentioned that you may have to change on a dime. For me, I personally have no taste for a sour beer. I will try them, but you would be hard pressed to see me walking out of a brewpub with a growler of it. I got a few requests for Wild Ales and sours at the brewery so I said "What the hell" and went for it. I open fermented my Saison De Beaver one summer and people loved it. For me it was acidic, sour, and not up to snuff...for others it was tangy, flavorful, and a have to have.

I would never have considered introducing wild yeast to a brew but it was requested, I met the request, and it was well received, even though I thought it would bomb. Now I will make a sour or wild ale here and there and find that there is a group of my fans that line up for it when I announce them. Go figure. Moral of the story goes back to my "Know Your Market" speech but also take into account that you may NOT know your market and have to change if you want to sell more beer.

Raising money

I have talked to nano-brewers that have done it alone, and others that didn't have two nickels to rub together.

I myself financed my entire brewery. That was great for me, I saved every bonus I ever got in my life and put it in US Treasury bonds waiting for the moment that I needed it...I never knew what I was saving for, but wanted some cash for when I got my "million dollar idea."

I'd say the best place to start is your bank account. You won't break your own legs if you don't pay yourself back. The next best place is people with disposable income that happen to be your friends and family. If your sister has 5 kids and works 2 jobs, don't ask her for money. But if your parents retired when they were 35 and own 4 different homes, feel free to ask.

You have to offer something in return though. It could be a number of things. Like beer certificates. If they give you $500, they get $500 credit for beer at your brewery over the next 5 years. It could be interest; it could be ownership in your venture, it could be whatever you want. Get creative.

If you have tried to get any type of loan from a bank in the last five years you'll know that giving your first born son as collateral isn't enough. And if you think you will get it for a business you have never worked in before and that has tons of well funded competition out there, then you're living in a dreamland. Unless you want to take out a home-equity loan to start this, you can just about forget it.

There are tons of resources on the internet that help you garner funds. You may find that there are craft beer drinkers in your neighborhood that would all chip-in $250 a piece to see you get started. Another nano in Pittsburgh did it, why can't you?

Consider selling some of your own stuff for cash. Do you have some gold coins your grandma gave you ten years ago and you forgot about them? Sell them and buy your kegs. Every house has at least $1,000 in items lying around that no one uses anymore.

Whatever you do, make sure you are comfortable with it. This is supposed to be a fun business. If you took a loan from Guido and you don't think you can make the payments in time to keep your knees, you probably are in over your head.

Some people will get their credit card and go hog wild to start their brewery. Again, this is not something I would recommend but it may work for you.

Here's another crazy idea...so crazy that at least 4 people in my Nanobrewery U.S.A. (seriously, you need to buy that book also, not a shameless self-promotion...you NEED IT!) book did it...they held investor tastings. They brought their beer, invited the community, gave away the beer, and then asked for money. It wasn't that easy but you get the gist. It worked for them so put that idea in your bag of tricks.

Space

Wait, space? What about the licenses? I say this because so many nano-brewers in the making want to just fill out the license and get moving. I can tell you that you won't get very far unless you have a space locked down.

And this is not as easy as it sounds. But since you have done all of this pre-planning that I outlined in the beginning chapter, you'll already know what you are looking for.

When looking at a space look at more than the rent...think of these important factors: What are the monthly utilities? Can I have a tasting room here? Is this zoned for this type of use? Can I get deliveries here? Will my equipment fit? What will my brewing capacity be here? What upgrades will I have to make in here? What is the cost associated with those upgrades? Will the landlord allow this? Does it have access to natural gas? Will people travel here for beer? Can I make deliveries to the bars I want to be in from here?

I would start with the local code enforcement or zoning officer when you find a space you think may work. Explain to that person what you want to do, and ask if it is even allowed there. If it's not (and I can almost guarantee it won't be), can you change the use? Every municipality is wildly different in how it handles new tenants in old buildings.

You are a light manufacturer whether you like it or not as a nano-brewer. This poses some huge problems in some towns; others are very easy to deal with.

YOU MUST DO THIS STEP BEFORE FILLING OUT ANY PAPERWORK FOR LICENSING OF A BREWERY!

This isn't an "I'll get to it later" type of thing. Find out immediately if what you want to do is even allowed in the spaces you are looking in. Some states and local communities have zoning requirements that Fidel Castro would say are too liberal and cripple growth.

I ran into this issue way too late in my process and almost got burnt by it. I had already been awarded my federal permit, and my state one was pending on this one tiny issue...the building wasn't zoned for that type of use. I was crushed. I had all of my equipment and was brewing test batches ready to go at the drop of the hat. Luckily local Patterson Township officials are some of the greatest people on earth and were very easy to work with. One month and $100 later I had my occupancy permit which was soon followed by my state license, and I was up and running. This could, however, have been a disaster and I REALLY don't want you to go through the panic that I did.

Again, I cannot stress this enough. You really need to check with your local municipality when looking at space to see where your type of business can be located.

Back to the details on space. Ask the landlord for copies of the heating bills if possible. Do you think you can control the temperature in this place well enough to brew beer? Find out the costs and add that to your monthly cost spreadsheet (I'll get to that).

Try to get as many cost estimates as you can and determine if you'll be able to cover those by brewing beer...or how much beer do I need to brew to cover those costs?

Assume you want the space and you are allowed to move in there. Your paperwork could take 3-6 months to get approved...work with the landlord and see if s/he will hold the space for you for no money down (maybe 10 free growler fills or something). Remember, they want the space filled just as bad as you want in there. Try and get a short-term contract signed if you find that perfect space.

I will say this and many of you will scoff at it...location doesn't matter. I have been to brewpubs/breweries in large cities, resort towns, and even a barn...literally a barn. I've found that all can work. Don't get caught up thinking you need to be on 100 Main Street to make it work. If your beer and marketing plan are solid, people will travel for your beer. I consistently get people from over an hour away to come and try my beer on a regular basis.

Another tip on your space...get it for free. You aren't taking up much space with a nano-brewery...is there an old building in your town that has been vacant for decades? Find out who owns it, they may give it to you. Sounds stupid but I actually used to GIVE AWAY property as a job when I was in the government. Well, technically we sold it for $10.

If you know where these places are in your community, a little bit of time and effort could land you the space for free. This gets back to being creative....or hardworking. Most times it doesn't hurt being both. Don't be afraid to think outside of the box.

If you still have respect for what I am writing (I know the chances are slim) you may want to skip this paragraph...still here? OK. Here it is...build the brewery on your property...5 months ago I would have said that's about the damn near stupidest idea anyone has ever uttered. However after writing another fine book, Nanobrewery U.S.A., I found that there were SEVERAL nanos that built their breweries in their own backyards. I know, it sounds crazy but it has happened so it may be worth looking into.

One other crazy tip…Your place doesn't need to be beautiful, just functional. Don't believe me? Ask yourself this, have you ever said – "The beer was awful at XXX brewery but the setup was beautiful. Let's go back next week!"

Equipment

No Licensing? I am filling it out anyway! I know I need it!

Here's a secret for you, you can't fill out the license _until you have the equipment_...seriously. That's right, you'll actually need the equipment and the space (or an agreement for it) BEFORE you do any licensing. Both the federal and state governments want you to have at least a shell of your equipment in place BEFORE you submit the application. Why? They want you to start brewing ASAP after you get your license.   And don't think you can be cute and just say you have it...they will want invoices for what you purchased and want to know what you plan on spending in total.

Before we get into specifics let me share with you how I am setting this equipment section up...when people come in for consulting I walk them around the brewery and point to every damn piece of equipment and tell them what it cost me. I also tell them to take a running tab and see if the number in the end is within their level of sanity.

I also tell them that I have confirmed I am not the worlds smartest person and there may actually be more than this exact way to create a nanobrewery...it may cost you more or less depending on which way you go. With that said let us continue...

I was really focused on costs when I started. I went for the most rudimentary setup you can find...a boiler, a mush tun, and a sparging station. I also went for a direct fire heating element. This was also with natural gas. The burner has 325,000 BTU output. I went name brand with all of this material. I shopped it around pretty well. I found there isn't too much price difference in between the makers of the boiling pots. If you know a really good welder there are people that have had custom systems made. This could save you about 30% on cost.

Stainless steel is REALLY expensive. A lot of your cost is going to be tied up with these damn pots and burners. You can expect them to range from $2,000 to $40,000 for a really nice automated 3 BBL System. Again, I went for cheap, but I also give up a lot...I have to do nearly everything by hand or pump. I am constantly lifting something and the work can really beat you up. I'm not being a pussy here either, I'm a pretty fit guy...I do 350 push-ups 3 days a week, can hold Warrior 3 for seven minutes, and I am still tired after a long brewday / cleanup at the brewery. (Technically not a shameless self-promotion of the brewery but will still count it as #3)

I have seen some very nice 55-75 gallon systems with pumps, hoses, temperature gauges, and burners all set up for you. These range between $5,500 - $8,000 and have been popping up all over the internet the last few years. Again, I spent around $2,000.

This is where that pre-planning will pay off. If you only want to sell growlers in house, have a small tasting room. If you are doing this for fun and not to make money, I would go small. You can always get bigger. Maybe a 15 gallon 3-tier system would even work for you. Those are significantly cheaper and honestly you can make them yourself. MANY Nanobrewers started on a popular 15 gallon system that runs around $6,500...MANY of those same nanobrewers immediately bought a 1 BBL system soon after telling me they couldn't keep up with demand.

If you want to distribute draft beer to bars, you are going to want to go big. You'll need volume here and can't have a batch go wrong, so invest in a nice system that will allow you to brew efficiently and quickly.

Next is fermenting. You can go a lot of different routes here. I have talked to some nano-brewers that still use the old 5-gallon plastic homebrew buckets to ferment their beer. Those are about $15 a piece. You can also go for nicer (and easier to clean/sanitize) stainless steel fermenters. These can raise your costs quickly. A 45 gallon fermenter can run you anywhere in between $1,200 - $1,600. If you wanted 3 of these your costs start adding up quickly. However this may be what you need.

You can also get larger plastic conical fermenters which run about $130 - $250 depending on size. 3 BBL Fermenters can range between $2,300 - $7,000 a piece if you go stainless.

Another biggie is bottles or kegs? If you are homebrewing (and I hope you are) you know that bottling 5-gallon batches sucks. Even with 22's you are looking at 28-30 bottles for every 5 gallons you make. If you brewed once a week for a month and did only 25 gallon batches you are looking at 600 bottles of 22's. That's a lot of bottles and a lot of space to store all of those bottles. Keep in mind you have to cap all of those, store them, and have a pretty large inventory of the bottles laying around at all times. If you think, "I'll just get a bottling machine," then you must have deep pockets. They run USED for a very small bottling line over $15,000 and up to $100,000+ if you want a really good one.

But bottles do have their advantages...once they are delivered you don't have to go and pick them back up like kegs...and they are cheaper. A pallet of bottles after shipping may only run you around $1,000. That seems like a lot, but that will only get you around 9-10 new sixtel kegs...

This brings me to kegs. They last forever, are easy to clean, and bars love them, but they are REALLY expensive for a nano-brewery. A sixtel runs around $70 used without shipping (if you can find them), and new ones go for around $85 a piece. I myself keg almost everything (I do 2 limited releases in bottles). I also own only sixtels. Remember, YOU will be the one moving these around the brewery.

I don't recommend sixtels for simply ease of use. A lot of the restaurants I supply beer to only have room for sixtels. They aren't moving the amount of beer a bar does but they want the craft beer variety. They are jamming 6 to 8 kegs in a draft system and don't have room for ½ BBL kegs. Remember, after you move it, they have to move it too! And you are the new kid on the block, they may not want to invest in a ½ BBL keg of beer from a new guy then sit on it for 7 weeks cause no one will buy it...they want the beer to move. Make sure your kegs have "D-System" tops so bars can actually tap your beer...I don't know of a bar that accepts corny kegs so don't think you can do that one either...get the real stuff.

You'll notice I am not saying where to get these or who to buy them from...I learned early on not to recommend specific people or products to people I barely know. These items are not hard to find on the internet and the prices are pretty stable from manufacturer to manufacturer. Do your research, find one you are comfortable with and roll with it.

Next up is the malt mill. Have you ever milled 50 pounds of malt by hand? I wouldn't recommend it. I also wouldn't recommend dropping $1,000 on a new malt mill either. Buy a hand mill, then hook up your power drill to it...you'll save $800 and get the same exact result. You can always buy MOST of your malts pre-ground, but expect to spend 1%-4% more for that service. Generally the specialty malts cannot be purchased pre-ground, but since you are not adding 50 pounds of Black Patent malt to anything it's not a big deal to hand mill a few pounds here and there.

Depending on your set-up and what state you are in, you will also want to serve your beer. I recommend a nice draft system. Find one where you can fit at least six sixtels inside; I'd recommend one that fits 8. This will make filling up growlers and pints much easier than some homemade setup. And they have great resell value if you take care of them well. These will run you anywhere between $1,000 - $2,000 depending on whether you can get a new or used one.

Don't forget couplers and CO_2 tanks as well. Nice couplers can run in between $25-$35. CO_2 Tanks can be anywhere from $80-$200 depending on the size you get and where you buy them from. Try to find a place that fills them up/exchanges them close to your home.

You will also need fittings, screwdrivers, hoses, and miscellaneous cleaning supplies to get started. I would put away at least $500 to this to get you started. Another item you don't want to forget is a nice pump or two. They run about $130 but you NEED this, transferring beer/wort by gravity takes forever and the pump will make your life much easier.

Keg washing: Yes you actually need to clean kegs. How do you do that? I personally do it by hand. It blows and is time consuming but is much cheaper than buying a keg washing machine. These can get pretty pricey. You can expect to spend $5,000 - $8,000 on a keg washer. They save a ton of time but the upfront cost may bury you. If you plan on doing the 3 BBL brewery and distributing to bars, I would recommend this. Your time will soon be worth the five-grand.

Don't forget storage; you don't keep your liquid yeast and hops by your furnace at home and you probably shouldn't do the same at your brewery. At the very least you need a refrigerator with a freezer. These you can find used for as little as $150. You will absolutely need this.

Also remember you need to store that malt. There are some smaller silos out there, but I would think you'll be using bags of malt and storing them on the floor. Please, don't put them directly on the floor; buy a few pallets just in case water/moisture get near the grain. This will save you from possible disaster.

Also consider a cold room. Not all nano's have this but constructing one yourself could greatly help with storage and any potential lagering you may want to partake in.

And when you are budgeting please don't forget to add shipping costs to your budget.

I know you have researched this big time, but add 5%-10% to your budget just to be safe. Sometimes prices change or shit happens and you need a few more bucks to cover your costs. You and your bank account will be glad you added the cushion.

Before you go ordering stuff, think of this: when the toilet gets clogged, what do you do? Stand there and flush it ten times hoping it will go away? Call your wife in? Call a Plumber? Take a picture on your phone and send it to friends? Or do you fix it? If it was anything other than the last one I highly recommend buying a nicer system that you do not have to put together, because you are also going to have to fix this setup somewhere down the line.

If you don't like fixing stuff with your hands go as automated as possible. If you don't mind it, save a few bucks and build your own system, that's what I did and am very happy with the result. You can build a brewery for almost any budget...if you have a fixed amount of money make it work. All in all, you can do it for as little as $5,000 if you "homebrewed" all the equipment, went small, and refused to buy anything new. It will take time, but it can be done. Just remember: it NEEDS TO FIT YOUR NEEDS! You may think 15 gallon batches will be enough (and it may be), but if you plan on selling your beer as many places as you can please get the bigger system.

Even a nice pre-fabricated system with 20 kegs and some plastic fermenters can be had for under $10,000, so you could get into this for less than a used car. Do your research, look for the best deal...please don't buy ANYTHING until you get prices from at least 3 different places, with the internet there is really no excuse.

Here's another tip...used stuff isn't all that much cheaper. I can guarantee you that your are not the only person reading this book, there are at least 3 others out there and maybe upwards of 5. With that information you can deduce that the market for used equipment is crazy and food grade stainless steel really doesn't have a price depreciation.

Again I have bought some used equipment here and there but it was more of a stroke of luck than anything...Final conclusion: Look for used but assume you're paying for new.

Licensing & some other legal junk

Ok, we're here...print out your damn state and federal paperwork and let's get moving. I am sure you were hoping there would be some 30 pages dedicated to this because applications are scary and this is the big scary government, they could send me to jail if I mess up on this!

Let me ask you a question...did you graduate from High School? Do you have a Good Enough Diploma? If the answer is yes to either, the application should be very easy. There are no trick questions on these forms. I have talked to brewers in other states and none have told me that their state's process was too difficult.

This will sound very simple but READ THIS and REMEMBER IT. _Answer exactly what is asked of you, nothing more._ If you are asked "How will you be brewing your beer?" and are given 4 lines to answer...just answer it. "I'll be using malted barley, hops, yeast, and water using traditional brewing techniques." That's it. Pretend you are talking to your spouse; quick emotionless answers will get you by without any questions.

A few other quick items that will make this process easier. Acquire an EIN number (which has no cost) and get a sales tax license from your state. You'll need these when filling out your license, it will delay your approval if you don't have them. By the time you read this paragraph you could have already got yours on the internet, it's that easy.

You'll also need the paperwork on how you are incorporated. If you have partners you will need an agreement with the application. If you are a sole proprietor none of this is needed. If you don't know how you are forming this company go to page 1 of this book and start over.

Another item to think about...look and see what is needed with the application. I can guarantee that you will need a "Brewers Bond". You are probably saying "this is impossible, what is that, I can't fill this out, I quit". This is very easy to obtain and since you are small it will more than likely be around $100 a year for a brewers bond. A quick internet search will give you a few dozen agencies that offer the bonds with a quick turnaround.

Also, do they want drawings, invoices, articles of incorporation? If they are asking for it, give it to them. Sounds simple...and it is. Don't fret over this. Running your brewery will be 100 times more challenging than filling out paperwork your 16 year-old would do in about 45 minutes.

Here is one recommendation...read the ENTIRE APPLICATION TWICE BEFORE FILLING IT OUT. If you have an honest question, which I had a few when I was going through the process, call the agency that is supplying the application and ask questions. Your tax dollars pay for some very helpful people whose job it is to answer your questions.

So there, your damn application is submitted, I hope you're happy. Since you did all the legwork BEFORE you submitted your application this will be easy and go through without a problem.

Before we wrap up this chapter I will even jam labeling info in here. This is something else I bet you have heard is a NIGHTMARE. Far from it. Maybe the easiest part. If you plan on selling and distributing your beer it will need a label, and not just the bottles. The kegs too.

Pick up a bottle of beer...notice what is on it...The name of the beer, who makes it, the style (could be "Ale" or "Beer", the city it was brewed and bottled in, the government warning, and the ABV (depending on where you live this may not be there). In short, that's what needs to be on your labels. To be honest I do most of my labels on my computer with a word processing program. Since I do kegs I print my labels on regular 8.5 by 11 inch paper and tape it right on the keg. No one sees it but the bar manager so all we care about is that the label is legal. The federal government makes this very easy via their website and you can submit everything online and expect an approval/denial within 5-25 days.

I am not harping on this at all, not worth the paper. There are guidelines, the regulating agencies CLEARLY state these. Follow them and you won't have a problem.

Also check what your state wants. Some have very easy labeling requirements...others are a pain in the ass. Some even want the ABV tested before they will approve the beer. There are also costs associated with how many brands of beer you produce. Some states charge you a fee for each brand of beer you make. Check to see what your state charges and remember to budget that into the cost of doing business. It may make you rethink that super limited batch you planned on offering...or at least change the price of it.

Knowing this, I would recommend that you have a few labels ready to submit while you are waiting for your license approval. You will want to submit these ASAP so you can start making/selling the beer as soon as you get your license. I made sure I had 4 labels approved by the federal government while I was waiting on my state license. This saved a lot of time and got me brewing and selling beer less than a month after I got approval from the state.

Now I know what you are thinking, this arrogant a-hole says it's easy, I have read 300 online forums telling me it is a nightmare...well, simply put it's not. To prove that to you here is an ACTUAL FEDERALLY AND PA STATE APPROVED LABEL:

Bottled and Brewed by Beaver Brewing Company
Beaver Falls PA 15010
Net Contents 1 PINT 6 FL.OZ.

PECAN PIE

Nut Brown Ale
Malt Bevarage Brewed with Brown
Sugar, Pecans, and Cinnamon

Do I have nicer ones? Yes, but this is a seasonal that I sell pretty much at the brewery alone and it gets the job done.

This proves that it doesn't take a rocket scientist or even a beer scientist to figure out how to get a label approved.

As far as "legal junk" goes I am not a lawyer, but I can tell you to do some planning before you submit this application, it could be a big deal down the road. Know how you are going to operate this business...are you and your spouse's name going to be on everything? Just yours? Do you want to do an LLC? Is this a Partnership?

You will have to know this before you submit your application because it is required before you can get a license.   Whatever you do think about it and talk with your partners in depth about not only what is expected financially, but what is expected physically with work at the brewery, especially in terms of time each individual will dedicate to the brewery.

Supplies

So you submitted your application and since you got that sweet GED a few years ago you know it will be approved. Your equipment is there staring at you, but you really need supplies. Where do you go? Probably the local homebrew store, that makes sense. Or maybe I'll order it online? Both are good ideas, but c'mon...you're a *Brewery* now! You're a big boy and can now actually buy direct from the wholesaler or the actual source!

All wholesalers will want your federal brewing ID (they don't sell to avid homebrewers) so you will need that first, but you won't need your state license to start getting your supplies.

If you are fortunate enough as I am, you live within distance of a wholesaler and can pick the supplies up yourself. This could save hundreds and maybe THOUSANDS of dollars in shipping costs over time. So see if you can. I make a grain/hops/yeast run about every three months and stock up.

I'll break it down by item:

Malt

Buy 50 pound bags. This is WAY cheaper than going to a homebrew store that may charge $1.80 a pound for your regular 2-Row pale malt. The wholesale price per pound ranges between .55-.75 a pound depending on where you buy it. If you bought a malt mill you could save a few bucks by buying whole grains, but if you want to save time you can buy MOST grains crushed. Specialty malts usually come uncrushed so you will need some sort of milling capabilities. Most grain makers say the grain will keep anywhere from 6-18 months depending on the grain and where/how you store it. So order what you can store, and what you intend to make without it going bad.

Look at your recipes, is there something you could change to have a less expensive malt bill and not lose flavor?

It's a worthwhile question. You could save some big bucks by substituting one grain for another...but if the beer will be diminished, that extra money could be worth it.

There is an easy-to-duplicate chart later in this book that will help you determine your costs for each beer.

Yeast

Same deal as the malt, get this from a wholesaler/manufacturer. Research the type of yeast you will need and make sure it is readily available from whom you buy it.

Not all wholesalers work with all yeast companies so do your research. To save on shipping (and your sanity) try choosing a supplier that carries all of your favorite malt, yeast, and hops. Also yeast can vary in price by manufacturer.

Check out what your favorite yeast costs and compare it to other makers...you may decide to change it up.

Hops

So your first beer is a Pale Ale made with Citra and Nelson Sauvin Hops...good luck with that. There is a reason you don't see that beer on the market, it's nearly impossible to get the hops for it.

This can be said for plenty of popular varieties. If it is a hop you plan on using all the time (let's say Cascade) you can probably get these at any time. Buying them when you need them makes sense. If it is the Citra, Nelson Sauvin, Galaxy, Amarillo, Centennial, or any other hard to find hop varieties (and there are plenty of them out there), consider a hop contract. This is a contract you sign with the grower/wholesaler of the hop that says you will be buying this amount (no smaller than 10-11 pounds) for this period of time (1 to 3 growing seasons).

When it is harvested they send them to you since you had a contract. If you don't have one, it could be the Wild West getting that hop. I know some small brewers have had to cancel their "flagship" beer or make it a seasonal because they can't get the hops for it.   This is also probably the most marked up item in the homebrew shop if you think you'd rather go through them to buy your supplies. Wholesale hops can be around .50 to .75 an ounce, maybe less if you buy in bulk with a contract.

And this issue isn't going away for at least a few years. Breweries are popping up weekly and you will just add to the problem!

If you are really crazy, consider growing some of your own. This is a trend that is picking up steam and great for making a Fresh Hopped Ale in the Fall.

I grow a very small amount myself and at the very least the hops are cool to take to tastings to show people what the real ones look like. (Shameless self promotion #4 coming up in 3….2….1….)

The Nelson Sauvin Pale Ale

Ever have single hopped Nelson Sauvin Ale? I highly doubt it. This is an elusive beer for even the biggest beer nerds out there. This is a hop that grows in New Zealand and has the craziest taste and aroma of any hop on the planet. It tastes exactly like white grapes and smells like a white wine.

I stumbled upon a small amount of these and brewed a batch not thinking much about it, figured my fans would enjoy a 1-off beer. And they did, way too much. This was easily the most popular beer I ever brewed at my brewery and I was getting a ton of requests for it...only problem was I didn't have any...and couldn't buy any.

I am sure if you type in my name and Nelson Sauvin hops online you would see 100 message board posts asking where I could find these, begging people to sell me whatever they had leftover...no answers.

I could have found the Holy Grail and no less than four actual bigfoot (is bigfoot plural bigfeet?) before I got those f'ing hops. After 3 months I still had not given up. This beer was going to make me crazy popular locally and I was determined...and I was promising customers I would continue it.

Long story short an Angel, well, brewery consultant with some ties, was more than way too kind and actually knew a brewer in California that may have extra...he introduced me and thankfully they were available and the brewery was willing to part with some of them.

I proudly brew the Nelson Sauvin Pale Ale regularly and my customers are very happy. I now have a contract so I can get them...that in itself was no easy process. You are a VERY small commission for a sales person. Buying 11 or 44 pounds of hops a year from them doesn't mean too much to their bottom line so they won't take too much time with you. Take it from me, I worked in sales, I didn't give a shit about a customer I was making $50 - $100 on. I did give a shit when it was $500 or $5,000. Do your research and PLAN AHEAD with your hops, you will be glad you did.

If it is a rare hop, and you know you will be using it, consider a hop contract. At the very least bulk up on it when it comes available and store as much as you can.

This story ended well but I put in a crazy amount of legwork to get this done. I wasn't lucky, it took work...and lots of it. This is an example of the "work" you will put into the beer while never actually making or selling one damn pint of it.

Whatever the item is, if it is popular and you can store it, buy as much as you can because you don't know if it will be there tomorrow.

Writers Note: I also wrote a 3rd book on Hop Varieties. If covers some crazy ones you may never have heard of, if you want to get into the gory details of hops like Alpha and Beta acids and what individual hops taste like then I would recommend the Hop Variety Handbook *by one Dan Woodske. I try and give a copy to everyone that comes in for the consulting...it gets the creative juices flowing!*

Running your brewery on Day #1

Your license was approved and you are now ready to brew beer! Awesome job, and you're welcome...all the advice I gave you made this journey very easy...

So now what do you do? I'll go into your marketing/accounting plan later, but I want to talk about running your brewery. First, how many people own this? Is it just you? Do you have partners? If it is just you get a calendar (or use your really-super-intelligent phone) and actually write down the days you intend to brew, keg, clean, and deliver beer for the next 8 weeks. Do the same thing if you are doing this with partners.

It is going to be a whirlwind of excitement, depression, awesomeness, and downright fear these first few months so I want you to have at least the shell of a plan so you can keep a pace for what you need to do and don't fall behind.

Will it change? I hope so, but when it does, reschedule. If you have partners it is a great idea to make a log of what everyone does at the beginning so you make sure everyone is staying on track.

I also want you to write down what beers you will be brewing and when they will be available. If you follow my super marketing plan you are going to have bars seeking you out demanding they are next to have your beer. You want to let them know what you have, but more importantly, when it will be ready.

Don't forget why you are doing this either. Remember in the beginning when I told you to write down why you are doing this? Remember that along each step.

What I really want you to do day on one is organize the hell out of the place. Put stuff where it belongs, clean what needs cleaned; make this as easy as you can. Having stuff in the wrong place will frustrate you pretty quickly and even more if there are 2-3 people involved. Have designated areas for certain items. This will allow you to sleep at night.

Marketing, PR, Advertising, Beer Fests and the Internet

I find that most people that want to get into beer know something well, that is making beer. Promoting it…not so much. Actually, of all the people I have consulted, none of them actually had ever sold anything.

There is a reason sales people are making a lot of money in the corporate world, it is damn hard work and not too many people can do it. I am going to spend a lot of time here and you may think you are smarter and have a better way…if you are…please use your method.

I not only have experience in selling beer…but I have sold construction services, newspaper ads, and was communication director for a politician…I have a bit of a track record here so this is the cheapest sales advice you'll ever get. The book isn't long…read this stuff.

Most importantly I have never spent 1 penny on advertising, I got it all for "free". You should get some pointers on how to get this free pub by reading the info. Consider this a guide on how to position yourself to sell your beer.

I will have a separate chapter itself for how to "sell the beer", yes…these are different things. I am going to break it down in several different phases for you starting with…

The Internet

I get approximately 30% of my customers via the internet...without it I wouldn't be in business. And this isn't just from my website...it comes from blogs, articles written about the brewery, social networking and everything else. The internet is more than just your website so let's look at each aspect individually.

Website

You need this. Does it have to be awesome? No. But it needs to exist and have UP TO DATE INFORMATION. This is very inexpensive. You can host your website and buy your domain for around $10 a month and in some places even cheaper. This also gets you a personalized email account.

Mine is Dan@BeaverBrewingCompany.com. Looks pretty professional if you ask me. I also don't care what your level of website building is...please visit my site. You'll see that there is nothing special at all there. It actually looks more like blog than a storefront. I used a template I found on the web and haven't changed a thing on it other than the content since day one.

Craft beer drinkers LOVE info on their favorite brewery or one they want to go to. The most frustrating thing for someone that wants to try your beer and finds out about you online is that you have no information (or outdated info) on the site. Nothing is worse than the first thing they see says "Come to our tasting November 11, 2008 at X Bar and Grill!" This may be the first time they run into your company, make sure you impress them with at least fresh content.

I also use it as a tool to let people know what I make, and what is upcoming. This way they can track progress and feel that they are growing with the brewery as well.

I literally get thousands of hits a month on my site and I distribute to a handful of bars. Why are so many people going? Because I provide fresh info, worthwhile info, and try getting as much exposure as I can on OTHER websites.

Are you having an event? Post your event online on beer forums and calendars for craft beer. Send your beer out to get reviewed by a beer reviewing website.

Don't overlook your website, this is a real tool. Craft beer drinkers are HUGE web users and if you don't have a site you are really missing out.

Homework: Visit 9 brewery sites this week. 3 macro-brewers, 3 microbrewers, 3 nano-brewers. Take notes on what you clicked on, what did you read about, what you disliked. Incorporate what worked for you into your own site.

Social Networking

For some of you this will be easy. For others it poses a real chore. There is no shortage of social networking sites out there but stick to the larger ones for now, Facebook®, Twitter®, MySpace®, and Google® are good places to start.

It's also a good idea to tie these into your website. If you post an event, new beer, or whatever type of info on your site, take the 2 minutes and copy and paste that info to the above social networking sites. There are no less than a gazillion beer social networking sites. Post your info on a few of them too and see if you get any business from it.

Also, add that you are on each of these sites on your business cards, cars, shirts, etc. People are moving more and more towards using social networking to get all of their info. Don't miss the boat on this. Some breweries go all out and post something every 10 minutes...others weekly...some even less than that.

Find a balance that works for you. I post to these sites about once every other day (more if people are interacting with me). This keeps me out there, but doesn't annoy people.

While I get very little new business from these outlets, it does allow my fans to know where I'll be and what I am doing with the beer. Think of it as a friendly reminder.

I'll keep my opinions to myself and let you decide for yourself but some sites are better than others. You may find after a few months that you get a lot of play from one, and almost zero on another. It really depends on your style and your clientele. Play with all of them, but if one is working better than another feel free to put your focus there. Don't delete the other one though; it may make a comeback for you in the future.

What I want you to do before you even start brewing is to create these social networking accounts BEFORE you submit your applications. That way no one else can take them...you may even get some people checking you out before you brew!

Advertising

No doubt when you open your doors 10 ad sales people will be hitting you up. I used to be one of them so I know how it works. You may be enticed, but like I said, I never spent a penny on advertising and my #1 problem at the brewery is having enough beer to sell. If you want, to be in the newspaper - talk to reporters, on the radio or TV – call the show's producer.

For the internet, you probably shouldn't be paying for it either. Are there local beer bloggers out there that you could invite to the brewery? Can you post to local websites that you are opening? Use those first, you will be surprised how much you get out of there.

Marketing

Keep a consistent message and theme...for everything. Whatever your theme is do it ALL OF THE TIME. Using the same colors is a good start. If your labeling is red and black make your website red and black, make your tap handles red and black, paint your brewery red and black, make your business cards red and black, t-shirts should be...you get the point. People will start associating red and black with your beer.

More than colors keep the same message out there. Do "you" reference yourself as "you" on the website? Do "you" want "you" to be the face of the brewery? Or maybe you want the brewery mascot to be the face of the brewery. Think of some successful craft breweries...some use the owner in all their ads. Others go for a mascot or theme like, fun or sex.

Whatever that message is...be it good beer, having a good time, whatever...repeat it until you get it repeated back to you.

Personally, I shake the hand of EVERY SINGLE PERSON that I serve a beer to and introduce myself as the brewer and the owner. I ask them their name and thank them for trying the beer. It's simple, but I want every person to know that I own it, brew it, and deliver it. I am going for the local theme where you know the people you are buying your goods for.

At every bar that I sell beer to I insist that I have at least one tasting at the bar where I come to the bar and give away beer for people to try. This works on so many levels, the beer drinkers meet the brewer, and for me I get instant feedback...is it good, bad, neither, what would you like to drink?

So what else other than a consistent message and look? Tie all of this together and incorporate it on your labels. I make unique beer, therefore I have unique tap handles...I hand make every single one. (Details coming up). They stick out from the plastic eyesores that litter bars across the country.

I can't say this enough...keep the message consistent, and tie it to everything you do.

Public Relations

You need to reach the region you serve by means of other than yourself. Local newspapers are a great start. They are always looking for stories to write. Same with local radio, so hit that up too. Most importantly, have a pitch ready for the reporters BEFORE you talk to them. Why is your story unique? Why do people want to read about this? The answer is not, "So they know you exist and buy your beer". Remember, the paper and radio station are there to make money, simply reporting on a new business is not news...but will you be the only brewery in the area? Are you focusing on a unique beer like Kvass?

Whatever it may be it needs to catch someone's attention. Also hunt out bloggers and larger regional newspapers and magazines that may have specific food and drink writers. Hit them up as they need to find a weekly or daily topic.

You can do too much of this as I found out...I hit up 3 newspapers, a few bloggers, and the local radio station. All of them did spots on the brewery the week I opened....while this was awesome, I found that I ran out of beer almost immediately. I wasn't prepared for the amount of people that read that and were excited as I was that there was finally a local brewery.

Wish I would have prepared more, but I did find that it wasn't a bad thing. The buzz was out there and it was actually good that I had to tell people there was no beer for them, now they had to have it.

Think of doing a release event. I did a few for local bars. I was there on hand as the beer was tapped for the first time and even gave some away as a promotion. That way the bar is working for you. It is a mutual benefit (remember those words, we will come back to them). Same can be said for restaurants. Is there a dish you think one of your beers would pair well with? Tell the chef and give him or her some of the beer to test drive. I have had my Basil beer on the menu a few dozen times, I would pay hundreds of dollars to get in front of that many people and the restaurants do it for free.

Beer dinners got a lot of run the last few years and this is another way to promote your product to a captive audience. I have done several and they are usually a good time that brings in more business to your brewery.

Notice that the money I am spending goes into the beer. I do give away some of it, but I'd rather have people taste my beer than see an ad for it. That first year I would say that 5% - 7% of what you make should be used promotionally.

Beer Fests

This is a crap shoot. I myself would not recommend them for a nano-brewery. Ask yourself a question...if you are opening a nano-brewery I am sure you have been to one so you can honestly answer this....did you ever buy beer from a brewery you discovered at a Beerfest? I have, twice.

Now if I factored in that I have tried easily over 1,000 beers at brew fests over the years the numbers aren't panning out.

Also think of just how drunk some people get at these, are they remembering your beer? Probably not. I have done several of these and I will give you this advice if you feel you have to do one...the smaller the better. I served 1,000 samples one day and the following month I sold no more beer than the month before.

When I do small tastings and events (under 100 people), I can almost guarantee I pick up at least a few fans. Because One: they remember my beer. Two: I can actually talk to them and answer their questions and Three: There is less competition at smaller fests/events.

And remember, people travel from a large radius to attend large events...you are making enough beer to serve your local town and the surrounding area. Focus on the home base first. Even if that person that lives 40 miles away loves your beer at the fest, they probably will never see it again so it could all be for not.

To make the fest a success, do something to stand out...consider making a special "Fest Brew" that will just be served there. This will create immediate buzz at the festival...trust me, I have done it. I had a 45 minute wait for a 2 ounce pour of a "Special" brew at one fest.

I have seen some brewers wear the same weird clothes, others wear bikinis...whatever you do I can guarantee you this, good beer is not enough. Stand out.

Shirts, Bottle Openers, and More

Some people start with mounds of shirts, bottle openers, pens, and whatever other brewery paraphernalia they can order.   Again, this is totally up to you but I didn't get anything until I was in business for 17 months. I put all my money back into newer and better equipment. I was also saving for a new building.

If you think people will want your shirts and you have the money for the inventory, by all means order away.

My one suggestion would be to price it fairly. Don't give it away, but you WANT people to have and use this stuff. If it's $30 for a t-shirt not too many people will buy them, and if they don't buy them you aren't getting any free marketing out there. If you have the items get them out there!

Beer Samplings/Tastings

These are generally done in bars, but I do a ton of these directly in the brewery itself. Now some states are goofy (that is kind) and don't allow you to serve samples in the brewery, check that out before you start. I easily get the most customers for my brand from doing this. The crowds are usually small 15-60 people and you can talk all you want about your beer.

If I had to choose one thing to do to sell my beer it would be this. What's a better sales tool than your ACTUAL BEER? There isn't one. When you have sub-par beer you'll notice by their promotions...watch a beer ad during a sporting event...more than likely nothing in the ad will talk about the actual taste of the beer. It will just show some dude with chicks with big tits and a beer in their hand. It does sell a lot of beer, but you are in a different market, so focus on getting people to try your beer.

I do at least one bar event a month and they are great for business. People like meeting the owner of what they are drinking and being able to ask questions.

Make sure you make yourself available for these, you need some personality to do them...if you don't have it, just speak passionately about what you believe in and it will work...trust me.

Wineries and Distilleries

This is a stretch but I have done a few of these and they worked. I teamed with a few local wineries and did joint beer/wine tastings. This brings in a unique crowd of people that would otherwise not try your beer and works for the winery just as well. Have not done one with a distillery but I am sure it would work as well.

Side Story...

"Gotta have great beer." This Is something you will hear a million times from the same piople that tell you doing this will be nearly impossible. That's simply not true. 85% of the beer consumed in the US consistently ranks at or near the bottom of beer review websites. Don't believe me? Look yourself. So why are people drinking inferior beers?

Three reasons: Price, Distribution Chain, and Marketing. Here's the bad news...You can't compete with them on any of those...not even close. But you have something they can't offer...uniqueness, good beer, and a local flavor. Embrace those because it is all you have. Taste is not the only factor when buying beer...I know you're reading that thinking (This guy is a complete moron), but it is totally true...seriously. Look at the shelves at the local distributor...how much of it is made by a company owned in the USA let alone your state or your community? Not that much at all. How much of it isn't embraced by the majority of America? Most of it.

With all of this said, I can't recommend making a really cheap extract-laden crappy beer; that won't help either. But don't take this marketing and sales stuff lightly. If you make great beer, it helps, but I am sure you have had a great beer from a brewery that no longer exists or has been bought out. It wasn't because the beer sucked, but they just couldn't get enough people to buy it.

Don't get caught in the trap I have seen other nano-brewers get caught in, the focus solely on the beer and forget _this is a business_. Companies exist for one reason, to make money.

Not to make a product or service...but to make money. Don't forget that. You may be doing this for fun, but I will say you still need to pay the bills and come close to breaking even. If you focus on the beer and never try to "sell it" you will be greatly disappointed. With that little sidebar, let's get to actually selling the beer...

Selling the Beer

Isn't that what we just talked about? There is a reason
large companies have separate PR, Marketing, and Sales
departments. Tell someone in PR that they work in
sales...duck right after because they may punch you in the
face.

I know a lot of you have never been on a sales call so here
are 7 things to do when selling beer.

1. *Bring a Sample*

Believe it or not, the bar owner/manager will want to try
your beer before they invest in it. Remember, that's what
your beer is to them, an investment. If it sits on that tap
for a week or two they are losing money.   Bring more
than one variety if you have it so they can choose one or
both.   A good follow-up question is "which one do you
like the best?" This way they have to elicit a positive
response. Bring more than one type of beer too. They
may hate your IPA, but love your porter, give them
choices.

2. *Go when they aren't busy*

Worst thing you can do is roll into a restaurant at 12:15
pm and ask to speak with someone. Go in at 2:15 and it
will be much less hectic.

3. Have a price sheet or business card to leave behind

There's a good chance the person you want to talk to is not there. But since you did all that great PR work they probably read about you in the local paper so want to call you back and get your beer. Give them a chance to do that.

4. Let them know how your beer will make them money

Again, they are there making a living and a bar manager may get paid on profitability of the bar. If you sell a sixtel for $50 to them this is an easy pitch. "There are $50 beers in there so it's a buck a beer for you. This stuff will be in demand since it's local and actually tastes pretty damn good. You can easily mark this up to $4.50 to $5.00 and walk away with $250 in one weekend night. They like to hear that. At stress it's only 50 beers. If it doesn't sell well, it will be off soon and they can get their "regulars" back on and won't be out anything more than $50.

5. Let them know you will be willing to help them bring in new people to their bar

Offer to do a tasting. Say you will post on all your social networking sites when it gets tapped and drive people into the bar (I do that one all the time, bar owners love it). Let them know you list on your site bars that carry your beer.

6. Guarantee it.

This sounds crazy...but tell the bar owner you guarantee this will do well for them or they get another keg on the house. I do this with every bar/restaurant I ever distributed to. Twice people said the beer wasn't a hit. They didn't complain, they just said it moved really slow and some people didn't like it. That was enough for me, I offered a free keg, and they took it and were incredibly happy.

One bar owner took the free one then bought 5 more and we did a "Tap Takeover" at the bar all week and nothing but Beaver Brewing Company was on tap. The other has remained a loyal customer. Neither of them abused it, and neither actually asked for one, but that free keg got me tons of business afterwards and they now designate a tap for me at their bars.

I know this will scare a lot of you, but if you are confident about your beer, put your name behind it. People appreciate that. Remember, you're the CEO so working with the owner is unique for these bars, give them something unique in return for them carrying your brews.

7. Tell your story

Please make your story better than "It's beer, you should buy it". My story is I am local, small, and will work with you so we BOTH grow our business. Yours may be that it is a Husband/Wife brewery, maybe you're the only local one, or your beer is gluten free since you have a gluten allergy.

Whatever it is, make sure to get the story in because that bar owner is going to tell it to his/her patrons so they buy more of it and make him/her more money. You don't want the story to be, "just drink the damn beer".

Most importantly, relax and just talk about beer. After a few appointments you will become a pro and be filling orders all the time.

Taxes and Insurance

Want to lose your license? Don't pay your taxes!

This is worth an entire page of the book just to drive home the point. It's important to pay them on time and fully. Please make sure that you factor in taxes to your beer when you are pricing it.

This is one of the first things people will think they can cut...it's the first thing you should pay...even before your rent. State taxes vary, but federal taxes for a brewery your size will be $7 a BBL.

(Writers Note: There is quite a bit of work in congress to lower that $7 a BBL to $3.50 a BBL but with your level of production that won't be that big of a deal)

Keep records on paper as a backup to whatever you do on your computer. You may need them if you ever get audited. It's worth the 5 minutes a week it will take you.

While insurance isn't required by anyone, I would get it. Most importantly, if you are serving beer on site, get liquor liability. Worst case scenario someone drinks a sample of your beer and then drives away and hits a kid in the street...they turn around and sue you because they were intoxicated and you over served them. Think about this one, not too expensive and worth it if you need it.

Consider some general liability and also some insurance on your equipment. Again, this is not totally necessary but can give you some piece of mind. Several nano's carry insurance (I do), but I have spoken to several others that don't. Only you will know what is right for you.

Lastly, have some "personal" insurance. What I mean by this is cash in the bank, have at LEAST 4 to 6 months of operating funds ready to go. This would be the MINUMUM amount I want you to have. If you spend every dime you have on equipment you won't have any money to actually "run" your brewery and you will constantly find yourself behind the 8-ball.

The Growler and the Brewery experience

I know in some states on-site sales are a no-no...but most states allow you to sell your beer on site. Several even allow you to sell it for on-site consumption (a pint). In Pennsylvania, where I am, there are some more than goofy rules and regulations. One of them is that you pretty much have to sell your beer in 64 oz. containers...AKA Growlers. You can also sell bottles in varying amounts.

You probably think Growlers are stupid, it's an arcane way to distribute and drink beer. I kindly disagree. Where else can you get 5 craft beers for $10? That's what is in a growler.

Here's something that will shock you....I sell over half of my beer in house. That's right, over half. Every time I talk to a beer drinker I don't tell them to look for me on tap, I tell them to go right to the source. What's fresher than from the brewery? Nothing. (NOTE: Since the first edition of the book I sell more like 85% of the beer in house)

I make the brewery an experience for everyone that comes in. I focus on the details...In the summer there is a case of fresh Basil displayed that will soon be going into my Basil beer. I do the same with Chamomile Flowers. In the winter there are malts and hops out for people to smell (and taste if they are really bold).

I have sheets on the beer so people can look at the calories, ABV, ingredients, IBU's and whatever else I can say about the beer.

I want not only the beer to be good, but I want the people to have fun there.

I also let people try whatever beer I have for sale, and on a month to month basis that can be up to 12 beers. Really encourage people to try your beer. You wouldn't buy a car before taking it for a test drive, don't expect your customers to blindly buy what you make. They will greatly appreciate this, believe me. You never know when you can convert someone...and if you can...you have a customer for life. They will remember that forever, the first time they actually liked a wheat beer, and you were the person that did that.

But back to the Growler...It is the most effective way for you to sell the beer. Think of all the costs that DON'T go into the beer when you sell it in house. Delivery costs, pick up costs, sales tax, tap handles, and the occasional "lost" keg.

This is the most profitable way to sell your beer. Whether it's in bottles, growlers, or drafts, you HAVE to sell it in house. It makes a huge difference to your bottom line, and it's the best way to interact with your customers.

Don't scoff at this, or say you can get by selling it to bars only. Name a brewery that you have been to that didn't sell on site and could? I personally can't name one. I am sure they exist, but for the 80+ breweries I have been to they all sold on site. They are either all crazy, or know exactly what I know and what I am telling you....sell your beer at the brewery!

To do this effectively you have to give them a reason to come in and buy from you regularly. For me I offer a new beer each month and many of these beers are brewery releases only and you won't find them on tap elsewhere.

I also conduct taste tests. This is from a test batch I do. You can't buy it, but you can let me know if I should make a commercial sized batch of it.

Kolsch Wars

Shameless self promotion #5 – This is one of the better success stories at the brewery for in house sales. I personally love Kolsch style beers. Done well this is one of the most refreshing beers on the market. It's also a style you can make that a non-craft beer drinker may like. There isn't an extreme bitterness or alcohol burn. It's nice and light but with some flavor.

Sales were pretty stagnant for two consecutive months at the brewery, and I noticed not many new customers were coming in. I thought I would shake it up and make 3 different Kolsch beers, sell them at Growler sales, and have people vote for which one they want in the full-time lineup.

My lineup was: Kolsch #1: Noney Kolsch – Instead of adding honey, I added honey malt to the one to give it a bit of a sweet finish. #2 Wheat Kolsch – this was a traditional Kolsch with a touch of wheat to give it some nice lacing and a thick head. #3 Imperial Sour Kolsch – I know, this goes totally against the grain for the style and some beer nerds head probably just exploded but I did it. I made it with about 8% ABV, open fermented it and added some bacteria to help it along.

So which one won? It was damn close but the Noney Kolsch was the winner so that joined the full-time lineup.

76

What I did find is that some people LOVED the Imperial Sour Kolsch. Most people didn't like it, but the fans it did have were rabid.

This also brought in about 40 people I never saw before. I promoted the hell out of it for a few weeks and it paid off. People really enjoyed that they could vote on the next beer. People love giving their opinion, so give them outlets for it.

Learn something else from this; try something out of your comfort zone to bring in new people. I had little faith in the Imperial Kolsch and for the most part and I was right, it didn't work well. But there were some people that loved it and have now become semi-regular customers. Others appreciated the fact they were able to try something they never had before and probably never would have.

Again, you can laugh saying that these were 3 stupid beers to make, but it is very difficult to survive on one type of beer. Even look at the larger craft brewers, how many beers do they pump out a year? If it's fewer than 20 I'd be shocked. People like variety, give it to them.

Running your brewery on Day #2

As you can see, you will have to manage every aspect of the brewery. This isn't simply brewing beer. It's a business (whether you want to do it for fun or not). You are creating a good and selling it...hopefully.

Remember that whatever your motives, this should be fun. You're making beer. Enjoy it.

In terms of running your brewery, here are 10 items that you should think about:

1. Keep records

This goes with the taxes, but also in terms of what you sell. You may love your IPA, but it may be 5th in sales for you. Track what you sell in terms of your brands. I'd also like you to try to track how long your beer stays on tap at bars. Easy way is to ask the manager when you pick up your keg. If they say 2 weeks, you may want to give them another beer to see if it moves faster.

2. Follow-up

With all your current customers, AND the potential ones. If someone calls you, call them back...not tomorrow...right then. If they email you, email them back...when you read it...not in 4 days. You'll be amazed what this does for your business.

I answer every damn email I get...even the 8 emails I get a day that say "Hey, take your valuable time to answer my 47 questions I have about running a brewery. I won't pay you or thank you but I'd like 3 hours of your time".

Yes, I answer all of those...You may have even written me this email once and were too embarrassed to follow-up to my response so instead you shelled out a few bucks for this book.

3. Don't sell beer you are not comfortable with

Make a batch that isn't up to your standards? Dump it. All of it. I don't care if you promised someone beer this week and your batch isn't ready or something went wrong with it. If you wouldn't drink it, don't expect someone else to.

If you are making good beer people will be pressuring you for more, don't put something out there that you are not happy with.

4. Always sell your beer

Overhear someone talking about beer in the super market line? Tell them about yours and you just might nab another loyal follower.

5. Keep your marketing fresh

Update your social media regularly...if you can't or won't just scrap it. Nothing looks less professional than a webpage or social media page that hasn't been updated for 4 months.

6. Accept help

You will be amazed how many people will want to help you brew beer...accept it. Have a bottling party at the brewery, let people come in and clean kegs, etc. People love beer and want to get it out in the market. I always find something for people to volunteer to do because I always have volunteers.

7. Talk to other brewers

Honestly I don't do as much as this as I probably should. Some brewers are in constant contact with others in the trade and they say they really benefit from it.

I much rather would spend my time talking to someone that wants to open a brewery rather than one that does. But that's just me. There are a ton of brewers out there that may or may not want to talk to you.

8. Talk to your customers

This is a must, the most important thing you can do. Their feedback is INVALUABLE. None of my customers request an IPA...so guess what...I don't make one. They'd rather have something unique, so that's what I focus on. Part of this is talking to bartenders...not the owner, but the people actually serving the beer.

I offer to bars time for me to talk to their staffs about the beer. An informed sales person will sell more of your beer. I always let the bartender know what is unique about whatever I dropped off so he can answer questions any patron may have.

9. Don't be afraid to experiment

I hate open-fermented wild ales. However I make them (on occasion). I did one with my Chamomile Wheat (shameless promotion #5) and it gets that funky sour flavor to it. Awful...but it has a loyal following at the brewery.

I added my Saison De Beaver to the open fermenting list this summer and it was accepted well too...last fall I said hey, this Roggenbier may be popular with some wild yeast...and it was.

Again, in a million years I would not go for wild ale, but some people crave them. There

10. Have fun

If this starts to suck...get out. There will be trying days, but the majority of them should be good.

This brings me to a very important point. People are going to hate you and hate your beer. Hopefully there won't be many of these people, but they will exist.

Take your favorite brewery...go online and start searching beer forums about that brewery...there are people out there ripping it...but how? Their beer is awesome! I love it! These people should go to Hell!

Everyone's' taste is different, and although you are a great person, there are people that won't get along with you and will take the time to rip you. It always amazes me that people have the time to do this, but they exist and will find you out there in some form or another and tell you your beer sucks.

I beg you, don't let it bother you. If you are talking to your customers you'll know what people think. Best way to tell you are doing something right is if people keep coming back for your beer. There are 1,800+ breweries out there and you are one of them. All 1,800 have their fan bases and haters. Beer drinkers are no different than any other people in the world...some are great fun loving people. Others are assholes. If you want to hear what an asshole has to say I'd recommend that you just fart.

There is no reason to waste your time fretting that someone posted online that "your beer sucks".

For them, maybe it did. Move on and keep making beer, that's what your job is...it isn't trolling the internet and convincing people that your beer doesn't suck.

Now, if you hear "your beer sucks" 500 times and no one is buying your beer, they may be onto something...but if your sales are solid and people keep coming back...just put that person in the asshole category and move on.

You'll need some thick skin to deal with some of your customers but I would say that 99.9% of them are great people.

Accounting

Unless you are an accountant and keep GREAT records, I would recommend software to track your expenses and income. This makes life much easier.

Also track what you make and what you sell on paper and keep invoices. You are paying Sales Tax and Excises taxes to the government. You can lose your license if they audit you and find out you didn't keep accurate records and didn't pay the correct tax amount.

I'm not an accountant and I highly recommend you use one. I'd like to talk more about tracking your costs so you can determine what you need to sell the beer for to make a profit/break even.

This is not hard and takes maybe 30 minutes to an hour a week. Just don't let it pile up.

This brings me to your cost sheet. You need to know how much the beer costs you. Here is a fictional IPA beer and how I would break it down...

Contents	Per unit	Amount	Total Cost
2 Row Malt	$ 0.58	40.0	$ 23.20
Rye	$ 0.85	10.0	$ 8.50
White Wheat	$ 0.57	1.0	$ 0.57
Munich 10	$ 0.77	7.0	$ 5.39
Yeast	$ 4.40	5.0	$ 22.00
Columbus Hops	$ 7.50	0.7	$ 4.88
Cascade Hops	$ 9.50	0.4	$ 3.80
IRISH MOSS	$ 1.00	1.0	$ 1.00
PA Tax			$ 2.48
Fed Tax			$ 7.00
Keg Costs		4.8	$ 4.80
TOTAL			**$ 83.62**

Plus Overhead

Equipment	$ 30.00
Energy	$ 40.00
License	$ 30.00
TOTAL W/ Overhead	$ 183.62
Cost per Sixtel	$ 36.72
Cost per Beer	$ 0.77
Cost per Growler	$ 4.08

I break it down by cost per unit, how many units and I using, and total costs. Don't forget to add your overhead! This is rent/utilities/licenses/equipment/etc. I also add a cost for the kegs themselves. It does cost money (supplies) to clean them, and I have a fund that I use to save for more kegs.

Again, this is a generic Rye IPA. Notice a few things: I could save some serious costs and not add the Rye, it's 47% more than the 2-Row malt. But if I want a Rye IPA...it has to go there. I also used some pretty inexpensive hops here to save some dough.

I divide the total costs by 5 (27 gallon batch makes 5 sixtels) to get my per/keg cost. Then divide by 48 for per beer price (account for 2 beers of foam). And my Growler cost is divided by 9. (It could be 10, but I usually pour off a few samples at the brewery so I conservatively say 9 per keg).

I could also add insurance as a line item, delivery costs, etc to get a more accurate read. To get your utility cost, add up all your monthly utilities from the previous month, and divide by the # of batches you do. This will give you a rough guess at what you are paying per batch and will help you with pricing. Also put your rent in there. I'll tell you why it isn't in mine later...

Really think about your beer first, then the ingredients second. Could a change of malt save a few bucks? Could I substitute in a cheaper hop and keep the taste I want? If it costs me $37 a keg, what should I sell it for? This is totally up to you and has to be your decision.

More Financial Info

Easily the most emails I receive from this book is about financial information. How much should I charge for beer? What percentage over your materials should your beer cost? How much should my rent be? What can I expect to make my first year?

My answer is the same for each question, "I don't know." I can't answer any of those questions without knowing what EVERYTHING costs in your brewery.

I will explain this in very rudimentary terms, I understand all of you reading this didn't go to business school so you never really think in terms of running a business. For you pros this may insult your intelligence, but still read it as a refresher...

I recommend putting EVERY COST you can find in setting up your brewery and writing it down on a spreadsheet. Equipment, Rent, Insurance, Utilities, Licenses, etc. This is your overhead. Now I want you to add 5% to that number.

After that make a round figure of how many batches you plan on making your first year. Let's assume you have a 1 BBL brewery and you plan on brewing once a week all year. That is 52 batches of beer.

Take that overhead number, let's say it was $25,000 for the entire year. Now divide $25,000 by 52...you get $481. So before you even buy materials, it costs you $481 to brew the beer.

Now assume you are bottling, you have about 180 twenty-two ounce bombers in a BBL. Divide $481 by 180 for an overhead cost of $2.67 a bottle.

After that add in your materials to each bottle. Now your overhead will change each year, you're not buying kegs every year, or fermenters.

That's why there are things like depreciation and 3 year projections and tons of other complicated things you won't find in this book.

Again, back to what people always email me about...How much will I make? It takes some time but you can't know what you can make until you know what it costs you to make the beer.

It also helps you figure out what you need to charge for your beer.

Maybe you find that you need to brew 3 times a week, or do only bottles, or only in house, or cut your costs by half.

I can tell you from my *Nanobrewery U.S.A.* book that people are doing nanobreweries for UNDER $10,000 a year, some are doing it at over $100,000 a year.

Bottom line, KNOW WHAT YOUR COSTS ARE! You will never be profitable if you don't have a VERY solid grasp on what your costs are.

How the hell do *you* make it work?

There aren't any secrets. I pretty much outlined exactly what I do and did to get this started...but I was smart. What are the most important items I would say added to my success? Here they are:

Rent

Keep it in check. I found a building owner that loved beer and had the space I am in empty for 7 years. I worked out a very reasonable deal. That includes me paying him some of the rent in beer. This took about 8 months to find but was essential.

Selling the beer

I exhausted this point, don't expect the phone to ring off the hook if all you do is sit there and brew beer...you need to sell it.

Sell it in house

This is paramount. It's the most profitable way to sell your beer and it really builds your fan base.

Be properly capitalized

It costs money to buy equipment, supplies, and cover for your mistakes. Make sure you have cash to burn after you get your license. Unknown costs will pop up here and there and having to put them all on a credit card will cause you some unneeded stress.

Keep it fresh

I am constantly changing up the beers I brew. If I kept it all the same all the time I wouldn't be writing this.

Generate other revenue streams

I never in a million years thought I would be a brewery consultant, but a few times a month I take clients through a 3 hour consultation at the actual brewery. We discuss on the phone what they'd like to focus on, then I work with them on that topic. I charge a small fee, (about 1% of what the other consultants charge), and they leave knowing this is doable or they scrap the idea. I would never have done this, but like I said earlier, I get no less than 10 emails a week asking if I will hold someone's hand throughout the entire process. As a way to scare people off I say I charge for it. And damnit you should too if someone asks. You worked hard to gain this knowledge, it's worth something! And like I said, if you don't, expect to spend the majority of your day helping people for free.

Also do personal tastings. Offer to do them at someone's house where you will serve the beer. I have done several parties and those go over very well. You add new fans to your brewery and you make a couple bucks.

You can also charge home brewers to use your "large" system to make a large batch. I don't do this but a few other nanos are doing it...kinda like contract brewing but on a small scale.

Get creative: you have something that is valuable and can generate cash in other ways than making beer.

One thing I do for a few extra bucks is probably one of my best marketing tactics. That's right, I get paid for marketing my own product!

Through the local community college (www.ccbc.edu) I teach two continuing education classes. One is *How to Brew Beer Using All Grains*, and the other is a *Beer Tasting and Pairing Class* where you try my beer and pair it with a bite of food. They pay me a small fee, but it brings in 25-30 new customers to the brewery 3 times a year. That's 75-90 new customers that I don't have to advertise for that the college pays me to teach.

They almost all end up buying some beer and they get to hang out in the brewery....and I get paid! It's a no brainer.

Find new revenue streams, you will be glad you did.

Tap Handles

Want to save $30 for every keg you distribute? Make your own tap handles. You may think this is impossible but you can make one your own for about $5. First you need the right hardware. I go to the local hardware store and get something like wooden chair legs or spindles. Cut them to the size I'd like (about 7-10 inches high). Give them a quick sanding and then a nice paint job. I try to pick colors to fit the beer. Then the most important part is to screw in the bottom insert so the bar owner can actually attach it to their draft system.

You will need a 3/8-16 thread wooden insert. There are about 15 places online that sell these for around a buck a piece. I get more creative with some tap handles than others.

After you have that done I would recommend buying some sticker letters, and a bottle of sealer used for kids art projects...put on your stickers to name it, then seal it up. From 10 feet away no one will know this was homemade. With the paint this costs no more than $7 a tap handle.

Yes they take time, but saving $30 a handle is worth it. Another plus is you make what you need. You don't have to order 30 at a time. If the brand of beer you make isn't a good seller, you don't want 29 tap handles staring at you.

People love the Saison De Beaver tap handle. I actually sold several of them to people that were fans (adding another revenue stream).

Bottles

I hand bottled all 724 bottles of my 724 beer...that wasn't fun. But it was necessary and created some buzz. A few bars that didn't have tap space were very happy to finally get my beer to sell. Bottles can open doors to new accounts. Some beers really just do better in bottles.

For example my Pecan Pie Nut Brown Ale was made for bottles. It is made with Pecans, Brown Sugar and Cinnamon. Run cinnamon through a beer line….now run something else…your IPA now tastes like cinnamon. Don't piss off one of your accounts by doing this. Some cream ales are notorious for this so use some common sense.

Some people go all out with the coolest beer labels ever, some simple. I've done both with (shameless self-promotion #6) great success. The Pecan Pie Nut Brown is a very fancy cool beer that just sounds like it should have a beautiful label…well, here you go.

As you can see, not too much too it…but it stood out so much that it went quickly…of course you notice the black and white label mixed in between 200 "fancy" labels at the local bar.

Either way you go track the sales of it...does one bottle sell faster than the other? If it does, stick with that theme for your bottles.

Last Call

So there you have it - how to open and operate a nano-brewery. You'll notice I don't offer any recipes or beer making advice. You are the pro on that one and if you need help there are hundreds of beer making books out there. I wanted to focus on the business aspect, you're already a great brewer, and you just needed a kick in the ass.

I also want you to think of something else; if you don't have a graduate degree (or any degree) treat this process like going to college. Do your homework (read this again), read other books, talk to other brewers, other homebrewers, bar drinkers, bar owners, anyone that will listen. Learn from other people but don't dwell on it...eventually you will have to look for space and actually do this thing.

That's my last bit of advice. Write a date down as to when you would like to start this. You have some timelines from this book, use those and pick a grand opening date in your head. This will motivate you to actually get off your ass and do something!

Acknowledgements

Thanks to my wife for telling me this was a shitty idea every time I brought it up. If it wasn't for her I wouldn't have planned as much as I did and put in the hours it took to make it work. (She has since changed her tone and now helps fill growlers).

Craft beer manufactures. If you didn't lay the groundwork for me this would have never have worked.

My family. My parents and sister had nothing to do with the brewery...but they also had everything to do with it.

And you! There is a passion out there for the nano-brewery...keep it alive and go start your own! When you are successful and write your own book you can add Dan Woodske to your acknowledgment section....

Some things that I feel are worth mentioning twice...

1. Thanks for buying the book!
2. Know your market
3. Know your costs
4. Figure out if you can put a brewery in the space your want from your local zoning office.
5. Add 5% to whatever you think your costs are
6. Be creative
7. Be properly capitalized, try and save money where you can but don't be cheap
8. Buy all your supplies from a brewery wholesaler
9. Create a website, facebook® and twitter® account when you get your name done, don't wait to start your brewery
10. Read this book again and take (mental) notes.
11. If you liked this book check out my other 3 books: *Nanobrewery U.S.A., Hop Variety Handbook, or Kvass: History, Health Benefits, and Recipes.*

Again thank you for buying the book, next time you are in Western Pa look me up and stop in the brewery!

Dan Woodske
Beaver Brewing Company

www.beaverbrewingcompany.com
dan@beaverbrewingcompany.com
twitter: @beaverbrewing